IMAGES
of America

RICHMOND TOWN
AND
LIGHTHOUSE HILL

The Voorlezer House Celebration on May 28, 1949, recognizing the house on Richmond Road as the Voorlezer House, dating back to 1695. Built as a combination schoolhouse, residence, and meeting hall by the Dutch Reformed Church, the Voorlezer House is the oldest standing schoolhouse in America. Following its use by the Voorlezer, the person who served as schoolmaster and lay preacher (literally meaning "the first to read"), the house was occupied for many years by the Rezeau and Van Pelt families and subsequently fell into obscurity. In 1939, Mrs. T. Livingston Kennedy purchased the house and presented it to the Staten Island Historical Society. (Photograph by the Staten Island Pictorial Service, West Brighton, from the collection of the Church of St. Andrew.)

IMAGES
of America

RICHMOND TOWN
AND
LIGHTHOUSE HILL

Margaret Lundrigan Ferrer

ARCADIA
PUBLISHING

Published by Arcadia Publishing
Charleston SC, Chicago IL, Portsmouth NH, San Francisco CA

Library of Congress Catalog Card Number: 2008924285

For all general information contact Arcadia Publishing at:
Telephone 843-853-2070
Fax 843-853-0044
E-mail sales@arcadiapublishing.com
For customer service and orders:
Toll-Free 1-888-313-2665

Visit us on the Internet at www.arcadiapublishing.com

For Meghan, Brendan, and John

Contents

Acknowledgments

There are many people and organizations to be thanked in the preparation of a book such as this. I would like to begin by thanking the Staten Island Historical Society, for the extensive use of its collection; Judith McMillen, director of education; Maxine Friedman, chief curator; Carlotta DeFillo, librarian;Kirsty Sutton, Jim Burkinshaw, and everyone at Arcadia, for the opportunity to work with them on this wonderful project; Catherine Cass of Crimson Beech, for the wonderful tour and an equally wonderful afternoon; Barbara Lipton (director of the Jacques Marchais Tibetan Museum), and Timatha S. Pierce (manager of public relations) and Larry Wingard (vice president for development), both of the Eger Group, for being extremely helpful; Reverend Joanna White and Gladys Barton of St. Andrew's, who were generous with the church archives and instrumental in locating additional photographic sources; the members of the congregation of St. Andrew's Church mentioned below, who have been exceptional in the help they have given to this project; Rabbi Nochem Kaplan and Principal Chanie Moskowitz of the Rabbi Jacob Joseph School, for their gracious and knowledgeable assistance; John Vurckio, who went to great lengths to obtain material on the Richmond Fire Company; and Bill Wolfe, of Wolfe Realty, who assisted in gaining sources for Lighthouse Hill.

The following individuals were generous in sharing their personal photographs and in many cases allowed me to keep originals until they could be reproduced: Jean Matula Anderson, who sent irreplaceable, annotated photographs from Florida; Edith Holtermann and the Holtermann family for their generous assistance and marvelous photographic perspective of Richmond Town; Oscar Michaud, whose photographs and reminiscences gave a wonderful view of Latourette; and Marjorie Holtermann Fandrei, who also shared many lovely pictures.

A special thank you to Tova Navarra, dear friend and colleague, whose photographic talents and generous contribution of time have made this volume possible. And not to be forgotten, my mother, for first taking me to Richmond Town.

Introduction

As a young child, I remember well the excitement of my first trip to Richmond Town. My mother loved Staten Island and thought it was the country. For a native of Brooklyn in the "pre-bridge" days—which is how many Staten Islanders delineate time—an excursion to Staten Island was no small matter. Before the Verrazano Bridge, the most direct route to the Island was via the 69th Street ferry, which crossed the Narrows at an angle contrary to that of the freighters and ocean liners headed for Manhattan or the open seas. On a hot summer day, traffic could be backed up to Third Avenue. Once in St. George, after several transfers on a public bus, there was Richmond Town. Quite an expedition, but one that was never to be forgotten.

Seeing the Voorlezer House, the oldest standing schoolhouse in North America, was an experience that captured my heart and imagination. It was there that I was introduced to an affordable type of the time travel: the historic restoration. The afternoon ended in St. Andrew's cemetery, where a kindly caretaker brought the history of the church and its parishioners to life. Every headstone represented a magnificent journey. I was bitten by the history bug in the way many people are bitten by the acting bug. From then on, I felt almost physically incapable of passing an old home without wondering who lived there, where they came from, and what became of them, and finally hoping the home would be preserved. On a recent trip to Richmond Town, I watched a throng of school kids follow a guide in period garb like the children of Hamlin after the Piper, and I wondered which ones would return some thirty years later to show their children the oldest elementary school, the Basketmaker's House, the Courthouse, and St. Andrew's Church. Richmond Town continues to weave its magic.

The history of Richmond Town dates to the 1690s, when it was known as Cocclestown, because of the profusion of oyster and clam shells left by the Indians who preceded the European settlers. It was a central location for the early Dutch settlers who farmed the surrounding area. In about 1695, the Dutch congregation built a house that served as a schoolhouse and home for the lay minister and teacher. The village grew in civic and commercial importance, and in 1730, Richmond Town was named the county seat. The continuing growth of Staten Island was reflected in the Greek Revival-style Courthouse (1837), the County Clerk's Office (1848), and a jail (1860). In the next few decades, the development of the north and east shores of the Island in close proximity to Manhattan began to accelerate dramatically.

While the north shore began to take precedence as a municipal center, Richmond Town went into something of a hibernation, conserving its energy for its next growth spurt. For the next few decades, it remained a peaceful residential area. In 1937, the Staten Island Historical Society acquired the Voorlezer House. A group of preservationists conceived the idea of creating a historic village, and Richmond Town re-invented itself in 1958, when the Society joined with the City of New York to create a living historical museum. While Richmond Town underwent its metamorphoses, the showplace of Latourette House had become a golf course. The lighthouse on the hill began sending its beam and soon had a new neighbor—the Jacques Marchais Tibetan Museum. Historic Richmond Town is a living museum, preserving and sharing history as it safeguards the treasure for the next generation. What may be most impressive is that Richmond Town and the surrounding area have been able to evolve, adapt, and add new elements while retaining their essential nature. Volumes can and will be written on Richmond Town and Lighthouse Hill, and I believe that the strength of this book and others like it is that one picture is indeed worth a thousand words, memories, and emotions.

One

Historic
Richmond Town

View of Richmond Town, a copy of an oil painting by C. Winter, 1851. (Special print from the Metropolitan Museum, collection of the Staten Island Historical Society.)

Courthouse at Richmond Town, a watercolor over pencil by Augustus Kollner. (From the W.C. Arnold Collection of New York Prints, collection of the Staten Island Historical Society.)

Present-day view of the Courthouse. Built in 1837, this lovely Greek Revival-style building is a monument to Richmond Town's importance as a civic and municipal center. Richmond County's Courthouse from 1837 to 1919, it is today the visitor's center for the restoration and houses the museum store and assembly room. (Photograph by T. Navarra.)

The Voorlezer House. (Photograph by Loring McMillen.)

Loring McMillen, noted borough historian, has been closely associated with Historic Richmond Town. An engineer for the telephone company, McMillen had a lifelong interest in local history and historic homes. He served on the board of the Staten Island Historical Society in 1932 and was director of Historic Richmond Town from 1967 to 1978. He produced a title for and established the authenticity of the Voorlezer House, thereby creating a cornerstone for the historic village. McMillen died in 1991 at the age of eighty-five. (Photograph by Jim Romano, collection of the Staten Island Historical Society.)

11

Mrs. Katt, whose daughter, Sophie, was married to C. Henry Holtermann, in colonial garb operating a spinning wheel in the Voorlezer House. (Collection of Marjorie Fandrei.)

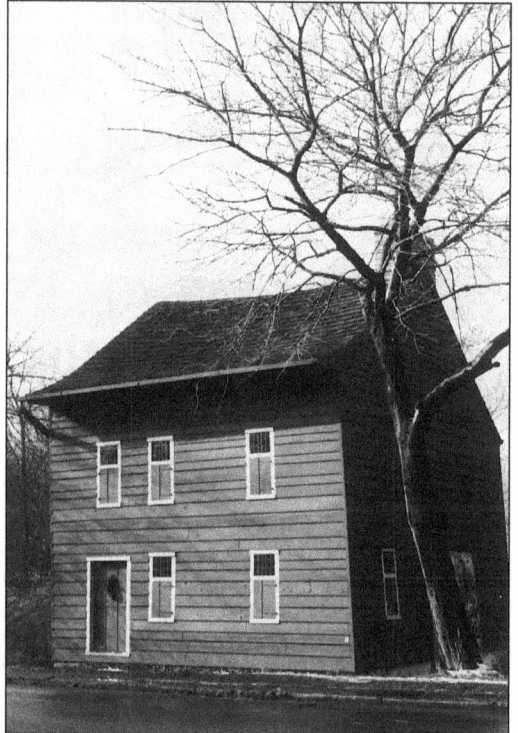

Present-day view of the Voorlezer House. (Photograph by T. Navarra.)

This photograph of the Voorlezer House with an "Eats" sign out front recalls a more pedestrian time in its past. For many years, the history of the Voorlezer House was obscured. In looking through old surveys, local historians began to suspect that the old house might be that of the Dutch schoolmaster. (Collection of the Staten Island Institute of Arts and Sciences, New York.)

When the possibility emerged that this was indeed the home of the Dutch schoolmaster, Nathan Rosenberg, whose parents, Samuel and Amelia, ran the house in question as the Arlington Hotel for fifty years, adopted a Missouri-like "Show me" attitude. On p. 13 of the January 6, 1937 edition of the *Staten Island Advance*, he commented: "I don't remember in all the years there any mention of that term 'Vorleezer' ... maybe it is and maybe it isn't ... but I would like to see proof." Nathan and Solomon Rosenberg are shown here in 1910, in front of the Richmond Roadhouse adjoining their residence, thereafter known as the Voorlezer House. (Collection of the Staten Island Historical Society.)

13

This group of Richmond Town neighbors at the turn of the century includes Francis Barton, of the Barton House; Charles H. Holtermann; Claus Henry Holtermann; Edward Marks (the gentleman in the center); and Katherine Holtermann (at the far right). The other woman is not identified. (Collection of Marjorie Fandrei.)

An interior view of the County Clerk's Office, c. 1895. (Collection of the Staten Island Historical Society.)

The Richmond County Clerk's Office was built in 1848, with additions in 1858, 1877, and 1917. This 1910 photograph shows a child in the doorway. The county clerk's functions were transferred to the St. George section of Staten Island in 1920, and the building became a museum in 1934, housing exhibits of Staten Island's history. (Collection of the Staten Island Historical Society.)

A *c.* 1910 photograph of the Carriage and Wagon Works. (Collection of the Staten Island Historical Society.)

Hooper Blacksmith Shop, *c.* 1890. The blacksmith shop was the eighteenth-century counterpart of the auto body shop and seems to have been a very busy place. (Collection of the Staten Island Historical Society.)

Isaac Marsh established the first large carriage factory on Staten Island in the Richmond Town section in the late 1840s. Marsh had moved from New Jersey a few years earlier, and by the mid-1850s, the factory produced about sixty vehicles annually and employed about twenty people. Ownership thereafter passed to John F. Schwiebert. The factory was also used as an auto body shop. It closed in 1939. (Collection of the Staten Island Historical Society.)

I. M. MARSH'S

COACH AND LIGHT WAGON

MANUFACTORY,

RICHMOND VILLAGE, STATEN ISLAND.

CARRIAGES of all kinds built to order from the best materials, and by experienced workmen.— Also on hand a variety of Carriages, Light-wagons &c. which will be sold cheap for cash. Second-hand work taken in exchange. Having been engaged in this business at Richmond for several years past, the subscriber has now enlarged his establishment and is prepared to execute all orders with great despatch, as well as in a superior style of workmanship. The latest European patterns are regularly received by him and may be examined by his customers at any time. ☞ Jobbing, repairing, &c. &c.

128 tf   ISAAC M MARSH.

An advertisement printed in the *Staten Islander*, July 24, 1884. The carriage manufacturer, the equivalent of the modern car-dealership, created what was a very important item for those who could afford it. (Collection of the Staten Island Historical Society.)

17

This intriguing, undated photograph, taken on Center Street, shows Mrs. Stephenson, beekeeper and honey maker, with a swarm of bees. The photographer is unknown. Perhaps he or she was stung and ran off in a rush. (Collection of Mrs. Edith Holtermann.)

Dobler's Courthouse Hotel was a busy establishment around 1900. (Collection of the Staten Island Historical Society.)

This photograph of Dobler's Hotel, taken on May 8, 1904, shows a Staten Island Quartet Club outing. (Collection of the Staten Island Historical Society.)

Mrs. Joan Hembrow, who rented the Morgan Cottage (now the Basketmaker's House) in the 1920s and '30s, snapped this photograph of her maid and dog. (Collection of the Staten Island Historical Society.)

Mrs. Hembrow made the following inscription on the back of the previous photograph: "My beloved coondog, Barry, with my dear English maid." The photograph was taken in 1923, when the cottage was originally located on Richmond Avenue in New Springville. The building was moved to Richmond Town in 1965. (Collection of the Staten Island Historical Society.)

The Morgan Cottage on its original site. Eventually, the cottage became known as the Basketmaker's House. Built between 1810 and 1820, it was a modest home for a small farmer and waterman. Today it is furnished to exhibit the lifestyle of a farmer/waterman whose seasonal occupation was basket making—large, sturdy baskets for oysters and small ones for berries. An interesting feature of the house is that the second floor is reached by an exterior staircase to save on interior space. The home has been moved from its original location in New Springville. (Collection of the Staten Island Historical Society.)

The Boehm House, built in 1750, was the home of the prominent teacher Henry M. Boehm (1819–1862). It was moved to Richmond Town from Greenridge. It now occupies the site of the Dr. Thomas Frost House, which was demolished in 1887. (Photograph by R.C. Fingado in 1978, collection of the Staten Island Historical Society.)

The intersection of Arthur Kill and Richmond Roads, photographed in 1947 by Loring McMillen. (Collection of the Staten Island Historical Society.)

Geib's Mill and the Miller's House, photographed by Simonson, *c.* 1910. The Miller's House was located at the foot of Old Mill Road and Richmond Creek. In the 1760s, a large gristmill known as Beadle's Mill was built here. The Crocheron family owned the mill from about 1800 to the 1850s. William Geib purchased it and subsequently sold it to the Simonson family in the 1870s. Destroyed in 1922, the mill was in operation until about 1900. (Collection of the Staten Island Historical Society.)

The Eusabia Johnson family, August 14, 1932. Their one-room store was moved from Eltingville and is now the Print Shop. (Collection of the Staten Island Historical Society.)

This postcard entitled "Bird's eye view, Village of Richmond" was inscribed with "Yours truly, Mrs. Dooley" on April 25, 1907. The Church of St. Andrew is prominent in the foreground, with St. Patrick's visible in background. (Collection of the Staten Island Historical Society.)

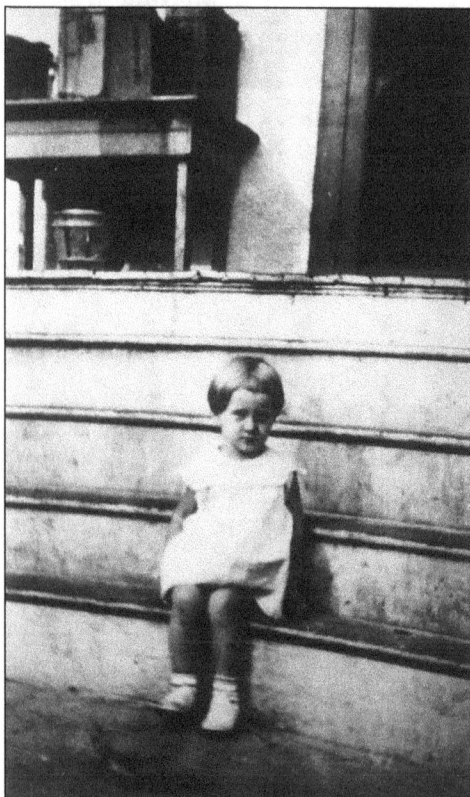

Adele Monti, born in 1930 and shown here in 1935, makes an enchanting picture—the wistful child sitting on the steps to her house, perhaps requested by her mother to stay put at least long enough for the click of the shutter. (Collection of the Staten Island Historical Society.)

The Guyon-Lake Tysen House, a striking example of Dutch Colonial-style architecture, was erected *c.* 1740 by Joseph Guyon. A kitchen was added around 1820. A notable personal touch is the inscription by Joseph Guyon of his name in an exposed mud and straw-filled wall. Originally located in New Dorp on 112 acres, the home represents the lifestyle of a well-to-do landowner. In 1939, when the house passed from Daniel Lake to his son-in-law, Daniel J. Tysen, it included granaries, cider houses, and a large barn. D.J. Tysen II founded Tysen's Tomato Farm and Cannery in 1885. The home remained in the Tysen family until 1932 and was moved to Richmond Town in 1969. (Collection of the Staten Island Historical Society.)

Bill McMillen (center), Al Erickson (right), and another unidentified man at the Bennett House restoration on May 22, 1969. Drawn to Historic Richmond Town by his father, Loring, McMillen has been involved in many aspects of Richmond Town since 1963. In addition to his historical expertise, he is accomplished both as a cabinetmaker and tinsmith. (Collection of the Staten Island Historical Society.)

The Stephens-Black House, built *c.* 1837 in Greek Revival style, was the home and general store of Stephen D. Stephens. Located on its original site, the house was part of the commercial and residential development surrounding the Courthouse. With a prime location, Stephens ran a lucrative business and, in 1860, he opened a post office in the store. In 1870, Stephens sold the house and business to Joseph and Mary Black, whose daughters ran the store until 1915. Willet Connor, a prominent member of the community, purchased the home in 1924. (Photograph by T. Navarra.)

The Treasure House, built around 1700, with additions in 1740, 1790, and 1860, has one of the most engaging histories of the Richmond Town homes. Initially the home of Samuel Grasset, a tanner and leather maker, the house has been used by saddlers, shoemakers, and bakers, in addition to serving as a post office. In 1854, a workman repairing a wall was reported to have been greeted with an unexpected sight: a cache of $7,000 in British sovereigns, presumed to have been hidden by British officers–hence the building's name. The Treasure House was also the Garrett Homan Bakery and later the first site of the Holtermann Bakery. (Photograph by T. Navarra.)

A worker busy at one the many restorations of Richmond Town buildings. (Collection of the Staten Island Historical Society.)

The Carriage Manufacturer's House was built in 1909 as a home and office for Mr. Schwiebert, who took ownership of the carriage factory after Isaac Marsh. (Collection of the Staten Island Historical Society.)

A Brovacone family photograph at the Woodrow Road House, *c.* 1925. (Collection of the Staten Island Historical Society.)

Bennett House, built *c.* 1839, with an addition *c.* 1854. Beautifully restored, the building was owned by the John H. Bennett family from the late 1840s into the twentieth century. John H. Bennett was a wealthy shipping merchant and the Greek Revival home reflects the typical lifestyle of an affluent family during the eighteenth and nineteenth centuries. Today the home boasts a collection of dolls and toys of that period, and, in the basement, the M. Bennett Restaurant, where hardy gourmet lunches and candlelight dinners are served. (Photograph by T. Navarra.)

"In the old Village of Richmond in 1879, there came a young man thoroughly trained and experienced in the art of baking, to begin what later has proven the largest establishment of its kind to have been developed by a local Staten Islander." So begins Dorothy Marks Heil's history of the Holtermann family. Born in the province of Hanover, Germany, and trained in Bremen as a baker, Claus Holtermann served in the military before coming to the United States. Here he worked in the Frederick Egler bakery on Bleecker Street in Manhattan and also in Jersey City before purchasing the Garrett Homan bakery in Richmond Town. Holtermann married Catharina Moehrmann, who bore seven children. Known as a kind man, during the Blizzard of 1888 he threw a sack of bread over his shoulder and brought it to the children in St. Michael's Home. (Collection of Edith Holtermann.)

The Bennett House as a bus terminal, photographed by the *New York News* in August 1952. Today it is part of Historic Richmond Town and has undergone considerable restoration to reflect its original character. (Collection of the Staten Island Historical Society.)

The adorable infant Jean Anderson on the hood of the family automobile. The Andersons picnicked at Richmond Town before moving there in 1934. (Collection of Jean Anderson Matula.)

A sketch made of the interior of the Basketmaker's House. (Collection of the Staten Island Historical Society.)

The Auto Body Shop, in an undated photograph. (Collection of the Staten Island Historical Society.)

The Eusabia Johnson Store, built c. 1860, was a one-room store that was moved from Eltingville. Presently it is the Print Shop. (Collection of the Staten Island Historical Society.)

The Print Shop now functions as an 1860s-style job-printing business. (Collection of the Staten Island Historical Society.)

The author at the Carpenter's Shop, a reconstruction of a typical carpenter's workshop, 1840–60. Visitors to the restoration are able to see in this representation a farmer, who supplements his income by carpentry, engaged in a variety of tasks from making buckets to chairs. The shop is constructed with materials salvaged from an 1835 farmhouse. (Photograph by T. Navarra.)

A rear view of the Carriage and Wagon Works, 1936, by Percy Sperr. (Collection of the Staten Island Historical Society.)

Members of the Holtermann family sit for a formal portrait by Bear Studio of the Stapleton section of Staten Island. From left to right are: (first row) Albert, Claus, Frieda, and Catherine; (back row) Willie, Henry, Freddy, Charles, and Katie. The third generation, brothers Al and Cliff Holtermann, started in the business at age twelve, working full-time, but their parents did not leave the business until 1976. Although Al and Cliff are still involved, the fourth generation, Billy and Jeff, now operate the bakery. (Collection of Edith Holtermann.)

The Holtermann homestead on St. Patrick's Place, in an undated photograph. Grandmother Catherine Holtermann stands on the porch. Her husband, Claus, died shortly before the family was ready to move into this house. The house was sold at a later date to St. Patrick's Church and has been the rectory ever since. (Collection of Edith Holtermann.)

A delivery truck at the rear of the second Holtermann Bakery on Center Street. The business moved to this location in 1882 from what is now called the Treasure House. By this time the bakery had abandoned the horse-drawn wagon for a truck, a 1913 Model T. (Collection of Edith Holtermann.)

Some members of the Holtermann family outside the first bakery in the Treasure House. (Collection of the Staten Island Historical Society.)

The Tinsmith Shop, formerly the Colon Store, built in 1840–50 in the Woodrow section of Staten Island. The store was moved to Pleasant Plains in 1913 and to Historic Richmond Town in 1969. (Collection of the Staten Island Historical Society.)

The Federal-style Crocheron House, owned by Jacob Crocheron, a Manhattan merchant. This residence was built in 1819 and moved from the Greenridge section to Historic Richmond Town. The Crocherons (also spelled Croshron and other ways) were a family of French descent and were prominent in Richmond Town. Lester Crocheron, one of the last members of the family on Staten Island, died in 1996. (Collection of the Staten Island Historical Society.)

A hand-tinted calendar print of the Geib Mill (formerly the Crocheron Mill), dated 1917. (Courtesy of the Church of St. Andrew.)

A view of St. Andrew's cemetery, prior to 1877. (Collection of the Staten Island Historical Society.)

A portrait of William T. Davis, historian and naturalist, born in 1862 in the New Brighton section. He is remembered primarily as a local historian and entomologist, and was one of the founders of the Staten Island Institute of Arts and Sciences. Davis wrote extensively and was the co-author with Charles W. Leng of *Staten Island and Its People*, a five-volume history of Staten Island. His book *Days Afield in Staten Island* contains wonderful descriptions of the plant and animal life on the Island in the 1880s. Among his many achievements, Davis enjoyed international recognition as an expert on cicadas. (Collection of the Staten Island Historical Society.)

The Guyon Store was built in 1819, with an addition in 1835, and used by James Guyon Jr. as a store until 1835. Later it became a private residence. Now it is furnished as an eighteenth-century tavern and used for special programs of the historical society. (Photograph by T. Navarra.)

Left: The Museum of Childhood, located in the Bennett House, has preserved a number of dolls and toys from the original town. (Collection of the Staten Island Historical Society.)
Right: A musket hangs over the "dark mantle," as it was originally described, in the Basketmaker's House. (Collection of Staten Island Historical Society.)

Richmond Road in a picture taken from a Barton House window by William Barton, c. 1900. (Collection of the Staten Island Historical Society.)

Lena Monti, little Adele's mother, in a hammock in 1935—ah, the good life! (Collection of the Staten Island Historical Society.)

The Gothic Revival-style Barton-Edwards House, with its Italianate features, belonged to Wesley Edwards, a prominent county government official. His daughter Ella and her husband, Willis Barton, a Wall Street financier, enjoyed the house into the twentieth century. This photograph was taken by W. Barton, *c.* 1900. (Collection of the Staten Island Historical Society.)

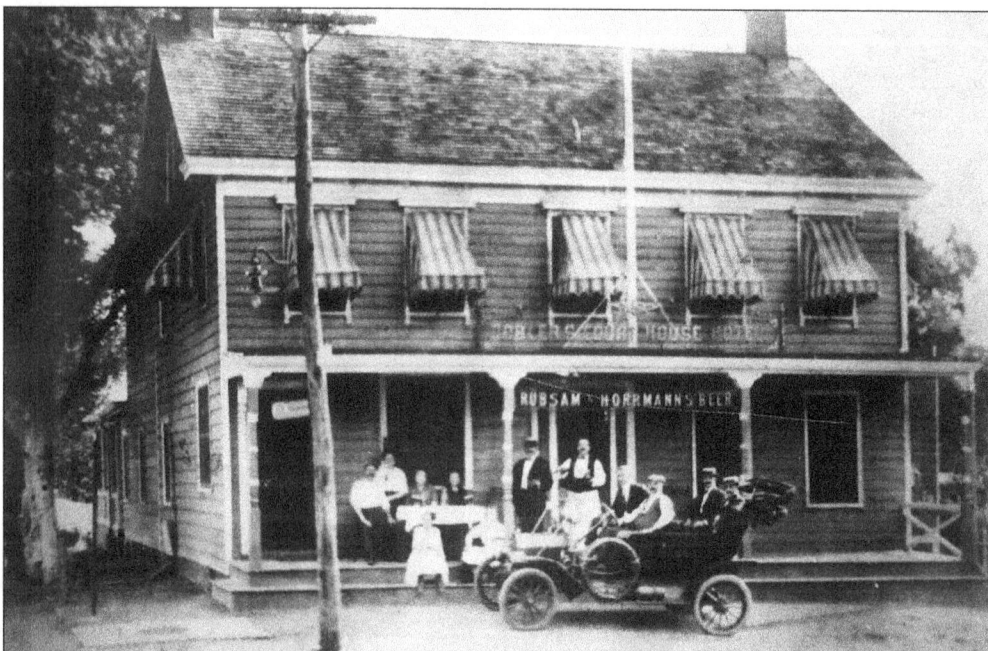

Dobler's Courthouse Hotel, of the early 1900s, welcomes day-trippers with its tempting Rubsam & Horrmann's beer and the perfect atmosphere for a rollicking good time. The ladies are also enjoying the day on the hotel's porch. (Collection of the Staten Island Historical Society.)

The Colon Store houses the Tinsmith Shop and functions today as a working shop. Originally it was a grocery store owned by James and Mary Colon and dates back to 1840–49. (Collection of the Staten Island Historical Society.)

The Parsonage during the Blizzard of '47, captured on film by Loring McMillen. (Collection of the Staten Island Historical Society.)

The Christopher House, built in 1720 with an addition ten years later, was a fieldstone farmhouse reported to be a meeting place for the Committee of Safety during the Revolution. The house was originally located in Willowbrook. A waterway behind the house provided easy escape in the event of discovery by the British. Eventually the house was moved to the Richmond Town Restoration. (Photograph by T. Navarra.)

Jean Anderson, of Richmond Town, recollects the 1930–50 period: "As a little girl, I lived in a house with a pillared porch that stood just a few steps across the way from the gravel driveway of the Flack House (now the Parsonage restaurant.). The two houses shared a circular driveway with only one entrance and exit onto Center Street. Their separate front walks went down more than a hundred feet to the road." (Collection of Jean Anderson Matula.)

Mr. and Mrs. William G. Anderson, parents of Jean Anderson Matula, pose for the camera. Mrs. Matula noted: "My father was in law enforcement and was honored with the Police Cross by the State of New York. Mother was active in the Red Cross, church and other volunteer work. My sister, Betty, became a registered nurse and is now Mrs. Oscar Carlson living in upstate New York." (Collection of Jean Anderson Matula.)

This beautiful, centuries-old beech tree stands outside the Courthouse as a peaceful presence unfettered by a changing environment. (Photograph by T. Navarra.)

W. Barton's perspective of Geib's Mill, c. 1899. (Collection of the Staten Island Historical Society.)

The stone wall in front of an old farmhouse located at Richmond Hill. (Photograph by F.M. Simonson, c. 1900, collection of the Staten Island Historical Society.)

Historian/photographer Ray Fingado worked for the telephone company and was active for many years in the historical society. His photographs constitute a marvelous record of Staten Island. (Collection of the Staten Island Historical Society.)

The interior of the Stephens' General Store, stocked with items typical of the period between 1860 and 1910. (Collection of the Staten Island Historical Society.)

The Eusabia Johnson Store, now the Print Shop, is shown here prior to 1910. It was also known as the Eltingville grocery store. (Collection of the Staten Island Historical Society.)

An oil painting of Hemsley Hall, the parish hall of the Church of St. Andrew, by Dow. (Courtesy of Lincoln and Mary Weidmann.)

This view of the Parsonage in the snow reveals a porch and dormers that were removed during a restoration. (Collection of the Staten Island Historical Society.)

The Kruser-Finley House, relocated from Egbertville, is a farmhouse built in 1790 revealing Dutch and Flemish influences. Additions were made in 1820 and 1850 to the building, whose workshop wing is associated with coopers. (Photograph by T. Navarra.)

A photograph entitled "Black Ben and Boy," by photographer W. Barton, November 16, 1889, at the back of Barton's home. (Collection of the Staten Island Historical Society.)

A modern view of the Basketmaker's House from the other side of Mill Pond. (Photograph by T. Navarra.)

Charles W., about twelve, and Marjorie Holtermann, about seven, in their Boy Scout and Brownie uniforms, respectively. The scout meetings were held in the firehouse. (Collection of Marjorie H. Fandrei.)

Townsfolk outside the County Clerk's Office, *c.* 1895. (Collection of the Staten Island Historical Society.)

Municipal and court employees, *c.* 1895–98. (Collection of the Staten Island Historical Society.)

Henry M. Boehm (1819–1862), a well-known teacher whose home now occupies the site of the Dr. Thomas Frost residence. This image originally appeared in Leng and Davis's *Staten Island and Its People: A History, 1609–1929* (Lewis Historical Publishing Company, New York, 1933.)

An engraved panorama of Richmond Town, 1860. (Collection of the Staten Island Historical Society.)

Richmond Town neighborhood children, in an undated photograph. (Collection of Edith Holtermann.)

St. Andrew's Church and creek, near the Hennessey and Washington Houses, possibly photographed by William Mersereau (the family name has also been spelled as Mercerow, Mushreau, and in other ways in church records). William was a member of one of the prominent families of Richmond Town and St. Andrew's parish. (Collection of the Staten Island Historical Society.)

Jean Anderson and Theodore Matula on their wedding day, June 30, 1956. Mrs. Matula said: "I left Richmond Town in 1956 when I married Theodore Matula, DFC, AM, PH, of New Windsor, New York, and Hawthorne, New Jersey, a World War II fighter pilot. The wedding was in St. Andrew's Church, a short distance away. Afterward we returned home to the Anderson House for a garden reception." (Collection of Jean Anderson Matula.)

Loring McMillen's photograph of Richmond Town during the Blizzard of '47. (Collection of the Staten Island Historical Society.)

A corner of the cemetery of the Van Pelt/Rezeau families. The Van Pelt and Rezeau families lived for some years in the Voorlezer House, after it was no longer used as a schoolhouse. Located a stone's throw from the Courthouse, some of the original nineteenth-century ironwork fence has been preserved. (Photograph by T. Navarra.)

A group of young campers from Brooklyn, in July 1972, listen attentively to a description of a carpenter's life during the 1800s. (Collection of the Staten Island Historical Society.)

The Hooper House, *c*. 1890, located at Arthur Kill and Richmond Roads, was photographed by Simonson. The people are unidentified. (Collection of the Staten Island Historical Society.)

A bedroom, appointed with a decor conducive to elegance, comfort, and serenity, in a well-to-do Richmond Town home. (Collection of the Staten Island Historical Society.)

The parlor of a home of the same era. The parlor, displaying books, family portraits, pictures, and accessories, takes on a more formal atmosphere than contemporary American living rooms, which are typically furnished with larger upholstered sofas and chairs, stronger lighting, and a large-screen TV. (Collection of the Staten Island Historical Society.)

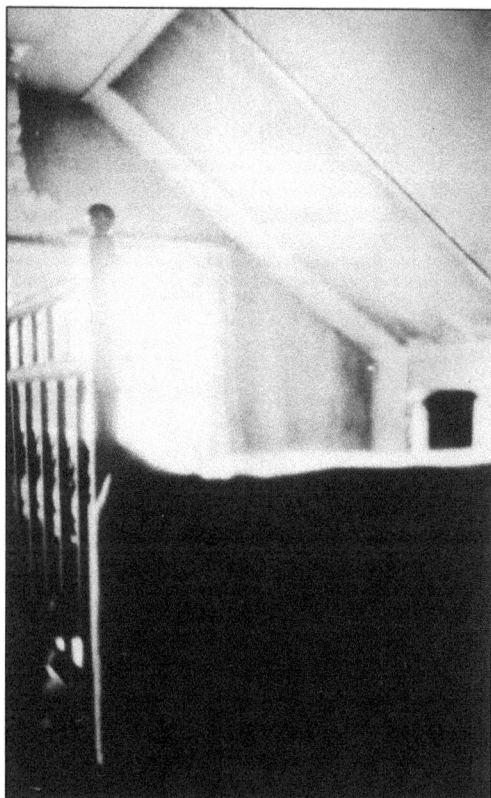

A bedroom under the sloping roof of the Morgan Cottage, 1923. The mattress is supported by ropes that had to be tightened nightly, hence the expression, "Sleep tight." Most of the photographs of the Morgan Cottage of this period are attributed to Mrs. Joan Hembrow. (Collection of the Staten Island Historical Society.)

The Annadale Store and Railroad Station, built c. 1850 and 1860 respectively, were moved to Richmond Town in early December 1975. In 1911 or thereabouts, the two-story trade shop and the station together became a private home. (Collection of the Staten Island Historical Society.)

Four adorable Richmond Town children, one of them Al Holtermann (upper left), in 1924. (Collection of Edith Holtermann.)

Originally located at the foot of New Dorp Lane, Britton Cottage was built of fieldstone and wood, c. 1670. The midsection of the house may have been the first seventeenth-century government building on Staten Island. Additions were made in c. 1755, 1765, and 1800. American botanist Nathaniel Britton owned the home between 1895 and 1915. (Collection of the Staten Island Historical Society.)

A gathering of Richmond Town children on July 10, 1930. (Collection of Marjorie H. Fandrei.)

The Crocheron House, a Federal-style farmhouse built in 1819 by Jacob Crocheron, prior to restoration. (Collection of the Staten Island Historical Society.)

Richmond Road looking east toward Egbertville, photographed by J. Irving Prier, c. 1895. Staten Island historian William T. Davis, in *Days Afield on Staten Island*, writes: "No doubt the present is quite as unquiet and wrangling as many a bygone year, but over the past there always rests a halo, and time, like a kind critic, idealizes for us the jumbled maze, and only gives forth a poetic tincture of the whole." (Collection of the Staten Island Historical Society.)

William Holtermann, who died before he was thirty, with a young helper. Marjorie Holtermann Fandrei's father, she recalled, used to say that after a day's delivery route, the horses would lead themselves home. (Collection of Edith Holtermann.)

The County Clerk's Office and Aquilino's Pizzeria, on Court Place and Richmond Road, photographed by Loring McMillen in 1947. (Collection of the Staten Island Historical Society.)

Geib's Mill, photographed by F.M. Simonson, *c.* 1910. Davis wrote: "A number of skirmishes occurred along Richmond or Stonybrook, in the years of the Revolution, particularly on the day of the fight at St. Andrew's Church. But it is more pleasing to think of it in times of peace, to see the water snakes glide in so smoothly, the turtles scuttle with much haste, and the wayward frogs jump recklessly off the bank, frightening the black-nosed dace below." (Collection of the Staten Island Historical Society.)

A horse-drawn carriage and a bystander on Court Street, *c.* 1890. (Collection of the Staten Island Historical Society.)

A graduation portrait of Marjorie Holtermann. She made her own dress for the occasion, inspired by the "Silver Thimble," part of the curriculum for graduation, and her mother's skills as a seamstress. (Collection of Marjorie H. Fandrei.)

The Edwards-Barton House, 1869, shown here as the residence of Nicola Aquilino. (Collection of the Staten Island Historical Society.)

A postcard of a German family celebrating July 4, 1910, on Staten Island. (Collection of the Staten Island Institute of Arts and Sciences, New York.)

Known as the Parsonage, this Gothic Revival-style building was built in 1855 and served as the home of the minister of the Dutch Reformed Church until 1875, when it became a private residence. It was also the home of Dr. Henry G. Steinmeyer, who was involved for many years with the Staten Island Historical Society and was the author of *Staten Island 1524–1898*. Today the Parsonage is a restaurant. (Collection of the Staten Island Historical Society.)

Marjorie Holtermann (second from left) and her little friends from Richmond Town. (Collection of Marjorie H. Fandrei.)

The Britton Cottage, on Richmond Road, during restoration. (Collection of the Staten Island Historical Society.)

The Christopher House on its original site at 819 Willowbrook Road, c. 1940s. (Collection of the Staten Island Historical Society.)

Two

Church, School, and Community Life

A keyhole picture of St. Andrew's by Burton H. Vernet, whose daughter Myna is shown here taking a stroll. (Courtesy of St. Andrew's.)

This 1952 photograph of some of the churchwomen of St. Andrew's was taken at a garden party celebrating the 80th birthday of Miss Vinnie. The women are Ruth Schaefer, May Rawlings, Judy Shaer, Elsie Boyd, C. Talle, Mrs. Halfpenny, Mrs. Dixon, Elina Salter, Alice Burke, Eleanor Roberts, Gertrude Maerschel, C. Osborne, Mrs. Guy, Mrs. Jessup, and Mrs. Ingram. (Courtesy of St. Andrew's.)

St. Andrew's Church in an 1936 photograph. (Courtesy of St. Andrew's.)

The chancel of St. Andrew's, in a photograph taken on Easter, 1909. In the background are the three lovely stained-glass windows. (Courtesy of St. Andrew's.)

Left: Theodore Irving, LLD, rector of St. Andrew's from 1857 to 1865. (Courtesy of St. Andrew's.)
Right: Kingston Goddard, DD, rector of St. Andrew's from 1866 to 1875. (Courtesy of St. Andrew's.)

Left: Richard Channing Moore, DD, became rector in 1788, and was succeeded by his son, David Moore, in 1808. In 1814, he was elected bishop of Virginia. (Courtesy of St. Andrew's.) Right: Thomas Yocum, rector from 1876 to 1904. (Courtesy of St. Andrew's.)

The interior of St. Andrew's at Christmastime, 1944. This photograph was taken by Weitzman's Photograph Shop, Stapleton. (Courtesy of St. Andrew's.)

Children skating on Mill Pond by the church hall in 1925. (Courtesy of St. Andrew's.)

Left: Rector Richard Charlton, DD, who was the maternal grandfather of St. Elizabeth Ann Seton, the first American saint. Reverend Charlton (1747–1776) was rector during the Revolution. (Courtesy of St. Andrew's.)
Right: David Moore, DD, rector from 1808 to 1856. Reverend Moore, much loved by the congregation, was rector for nearly fifty years. (Courtesy of St. Andrew's.)

Almost since the beginning of European settlement on Staten Island, the Church of St. Andrew has been a peaceful presence in Richmond Town. Established in 1709, the church received its royal charter from Queen Anne in 1712, and the charter is still in the possession of the church today. During the Revolution, the church served as headquarters for British officers who relinquished it for Sunday services. The church has suffered two separate fires, and, like the phoenix, seemed only to rise to become stronger. In addition to the lovely Romanesque

church built in 1872 upon the foundation of the earlier church, St. Andrew's is notable for its historic cemetery. Although it lies outside the boundaries of Historic Richmond Town, it is an integral part of Richmond Town and continues to serve a very active Episcopal congregation. St. Andrew's is a registered New York City landmark. The first rector was Aeneas McKenzie, who arrived in 1710. (Photograph by T. Navarra.)

A receipt for a pew received from John Wright for the sum of £9 in 1796. The wardens of the church are noted as Lawrence Hillyer and Peter Mersereau. (Courtesy of St. Andrew's.)

This view of Richmond Town, dated July 16, 1898, was taken by George Heck of Prince's Bay. (Courtesy of St. Andrew's.)

The 1948 Pageant at St. Andrew's. In this photograph are Ernest Salter, Gerard Schaefer, William Smith, and Patricia Hobson. One young lady is unidentified. (Courtesy of St. Andrew's.)

The burial place of St. Elizabeth Seton's grandparents, parents, and sister. Her grandfather, Reverend Richard Charlton, was rector during the Revolution. A convert to Catholicism, in 1975 Mother Seton became the first native-born American to be canonized and declared a saint by the Roman Catholic Church. Born in 1774, she married William Magee Seton and had five children. Following her husband's death in 1803, Elizabeth Seton became a Catholic and opened an elementary school in Baltimore, Maryland. She is credited with beginning the parochial school system in the U.S. and founding the first American religious order, the Sisters of Charity of St. Joseph. (Photograph by T. Navarra.)

The gravestone of Captain James Hart bears the following inscription: "Born Virginia, March 17, 1792. Died on Staten Island, February 24, 1864. 'Thy barque which many stormy waves have cross'd And threatening billows impetuously have toss'd, Is safe arrived, in heaven, its destined home, Where winds and waves can never, never come.' (Photograph by T. Navarra.)

An Angel of Death headstone, a well-known motif in colonial cemeteries. It was less harsh a symbol than the earlier skull-and-crossbones. Both types of carving are present at St. Andrew's and are well-documented by a study by the N.Y.C. Landmark Commission. Although both these designs are distributed among those of English, Dutch, and French extraction, a floral motif seems used only by those with French or Dutch surnames. The work of a well-known Manhattan carver of the period, John Zurichen, whose work can also be seen in Trinity Church in lower Manhattan, is present. (Photograph by T. Navarra.)

The Voorlezer House Celebration on May 28, 1939. (Courtesy of St. Andrew's.)

A woodblock print of the Old Town Bridge, constructed in 1845. It replaced an earlier wooden bridge over Richmond Creek along the road connecting the northern parts of Staten Island with the south. It is the only surviving example of an arch bridge on the Island. (Block courtesy of St. Andrew's, print by T. Navarra.)

A brownstone headstone with an Angel of Death motif over the grave of "Docter Oliver Taylor, who departed this life August 5th, 1771." (Photograph by T. Navarra.)

Some boys atop the hill, making ready to ride their sleds downward as fast as they can go, in a *c.* 1900 photograph by Barton. St. Patrick's Church can be seen from the hill. (Courtesy of St. Andrew's.)

Left: Oscar F. Moore, DD, rector from 1920 to 1929. (Courtesy of St. Andrew's.)
Right: Reverend F.R. Godolphin, rector of St. Andrew's. (Courtesy of St. Andrew's.)

St. Andrew's choir, in an undated photograph. (Collection of Jean Anderson Matula.)

The cover sheet of a song written especially for St. Andrew's Church. (Courtesy of St. Andrew's.)

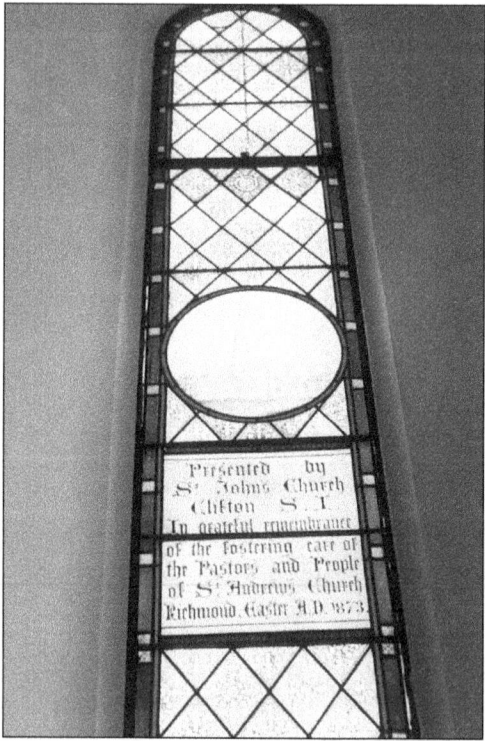

The stained-glass window, with a panoramic depiction of the church in the circular inset, given to St. Andrew's by the congregation of St. John's in Clifton in 1873. (Photograph by T. Navarra.)

This is not a full length row; it commences at the north-west corner of the Siddall lot.

142   In memory of Mary A. Crocheron, who died Feb. 2, 1848, AE. 41 years, 7 mo's. & 12 d's.

> Hark! from the tomb a mournful sound,
>   My ears attend the cry,
> Ye living men come view the ground,
>   Where you must shortly lie.

143   In Memory of Abraham Crocheron who died Nov. 13, 1842, aged 78 y'rs 9 m. & 10 d's.

> Unveil thy bosom faithful tomb,
>   Take this new treasure to thy trust
> And give these sacred relics room
>   To slumber in the silent dust.

144   In memory of Mary, wife of Abraham Crocheron, who died Oct. 1, 1843, AE. 74 y'rs. 5 mo's. & 9 d's.

> Receive, O earth her faded form,
>   In thy cold bosom let it lie;
> Here let it rest from every storm,
>   Till it shall rise no more to die.

145   In memory of Cornelius Crocheron who died Nov. 22, 1845, AE. 50 y'rs. 6 mo's. & 16 d's.

> Behold at evening tide trouble;
> and before the morning he is
> not.   Isaiah XVII 14.

146   In memory of Sarah, relict of Cornelius Crocheron, who died April 20, 1878, AE. 83 y'rs. & 2 mo's.

> "I know that my redeemer liveth, and
> that He shall stand at the latter day
> upon the earth: And though after my
> skin, worms destroy this body, yet in
> my flesh, shall I see God."

A listing of some of the sixth row of gravestones in St. Andrew's cemetery, from Davis, Leng, and Bosburgh's history of St. Andrew's Church. The listing includes not only the names and dates of birth and death, but also the inscriptions on the headstones. This excerpt lists several members of the Crocheron family.

A 1920 postcard of St. Patrick's Church and rectory, with a picture of Reverend C.J. Parks on the occasion of his Silver Jubilee. The back of the card, dated Christmas, 1920, is addressed to Mr. Albert Holtermann and signed by Reverend Parks. (Courtesy of St. Andrew's.)

The plaque in this photograph reads: St. Patrick's Church is representative of the Romanesque Revival style of architecture. Built in 1862, it has remained relatively unaltered since it was completed. Its light-colored brick walls provide an effective contrast to the dark brown doorway and, indeed, the charm of this simple building depends largely on the interesting play of light and shadow on its smooth walls. The 19th century wrought-iron lamps which flank the entrance lend distinction to the structure.

Public School 28, built in 1908 to replace the one-room schoolhouse that served the village of Richmond Town. This lovely Romanesque building was used as a school until the late 1970s. (Photograph by T. Navarra.)

St. Patrick's Church, built 1860–1862, is a registered New York City landmark. The church, a lovely brick building, was painted white at one time. Luckily, the paint was eventually removed and the brickface restored. St. Patrick's enjoys an active congregation and parochial school. (Photograph by T. Navarra.)

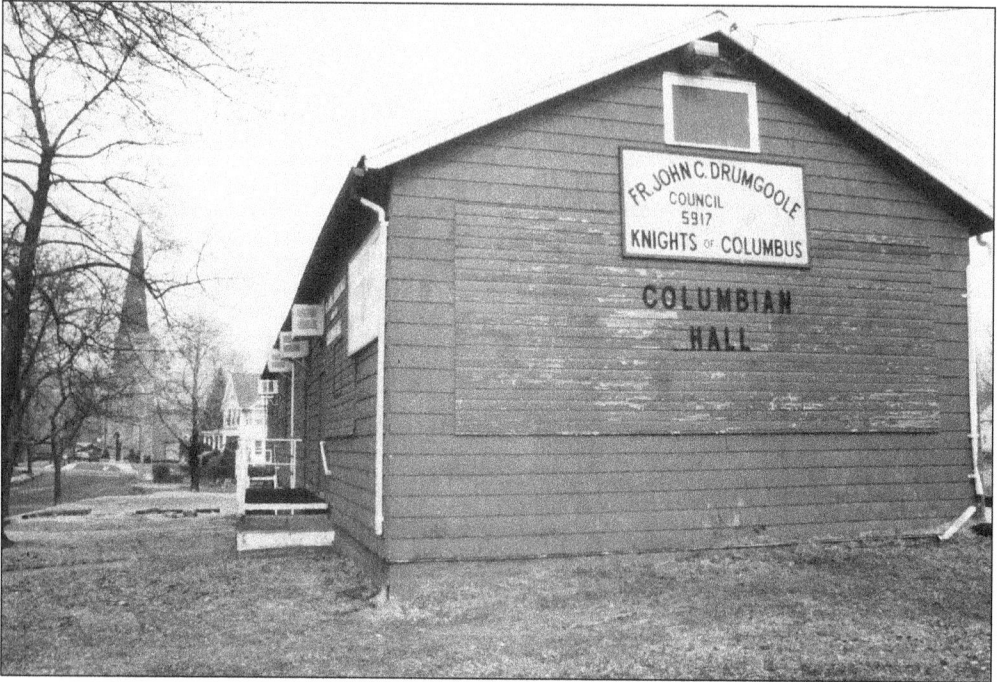

Columbian Hall serves as meeting place for the Knights of Columbus of St. Patrick's parish. The church is at the far left and the rectory can be seen between it and the hall. (Photograph by T. Navarra.)

The elementary school serves St. Patrick's parish. Built in the early 1960s, it has a banner that reads: "St. Patrick's School, Middle States Accredited, A School You Can Believe In." (Photograph by T. Navarra.)

The front entrance of the convent of St. Patrick's parish in Richmond Town. (Photograph by T. Navarra.)

Music teacher Mrs. Virginia Fisher (top left), Principal John J. Richards (top center), and eighth-grade teacher Florence Childs (top right) pose with their students at a PS 28 event. Included in this photograph are: (front row) Mary Iaturo, Rose Pistilli, Dicky Stanley, and Alice Stack; (middle row) Edith Benditti, Joan Vosburgh, Marjorie Holtermann, and Jean Elliot. (Collection of Marjorie H. Fandrei.)

An eighth-grade graduation at PS 28. Included in this photograph are: (front row) Mary Iaturo, Anthony Cirelli, Mary Desecio, Charles Klein, and Marjorie Holtermann; (back row) John J. Richards (far left), Michael Petrangelo, Clifford Holtermann, Lawrence Hill, and teacher Florence Childs. (Collection of Marjorie H. Fandrei.)

PS 23 was the public school which replaced PS 28 because of the growing population of the area. The school is noted for its high level of academic achievement. (Photograph by T. Navarra.)

Oded Karity, a student at the Rabbi Jacob Joseph School, stands happily at the front entrance to the Richmond Road building acquired by Young Israel for the boys' yeshiva. (Photograph by T. Navarra.)

Joshua Abraham, Yitzchak Katz, Yehuda Farkas, Avrum Bram, C. Mark, and Brian Bergson are some of the kindergarten boys at the Rabbi Jacob Joseph School in this 1994 photograph. (Courtesy of the Rabbi Jacob Joseph School.)

Rabbi Friedman, who was the third principal of the yeshiva and enjoyed a tenure of ten years, talks to two preschoolers. (Courtesy of the Rabbi Jacob Joseph School.)

GRADUATES • 5741

The graduating class of the Jewish Year 5741. The school was formed in 1978 in response to the growing population of the Young Israel Orthodox Jewish community in the Willowbrook section of Staten Island. Initially, families were carpooling their children to Brooklyn in order for them to receive a yeshiva education. Rabbi Jay Marcus helped the young families found the Rabbi Jacob Joseph School in Richmond Town. (Courtesy of the Rabbi Jacob Joseph School.)

This portrait of Rabbi Jacob Joseph, for whom the yeshiva was named, is a detail from a larger engraving. The engraving includes the picture of an open book, in which is written in Hebrew: "The more one studies the Torah, the more fully one lives. The actions of this world will be rewarded in the world to come." Rabbi Jacob Joseph, of the Lower East Side of New York City, believed that many Jewish cultural and religious values were being lost and felt the need to establish a school that would teach these traditional values. Although this was not realized in his lifetime, the first yeshiva—a Jewish day school providing secular and religious instruction—was built on Henry Street on the Lower East Side and named for him. (Courtesy of the Rabbi Jacob Joseph School.)

A graduation picture with Rabbi Nochem Kaplan (far left) and Chanie Moskowitz, principal of academic studies, at the far right. Mrs. Moskowitz said she viewed the school's philosophy as being a "suspension rather than a solution" by teaching the value of retaining traditional Jewish culture while living in a diverse, secular world. (Courtesy of the Rabbi Jacob Joseph School.)

Catherine Cass, owner of the home known as "Crimson Beech," designed by American architect Frank Lloyd Wright (1867–1959), stands unsmiling with her family. From the time she was a little girl, Mrs. Cass's mother told her not to smile because she had the notion that to smile was to appear foolish and unrefined. (Courtesy of Catherine Cass.)

John W. Vurckio, of Clarke Avenue, a fire chief and president of the Richmond Engine Company No. 1 for twenty years and a member of the company for more than sixty years. A lifelong resident of Richmond Town and one of seven siblings, Vurckio worked as a foreman of a construction company and exemplifies community involvement at its most dedicated. Past fire chiefs include C. Henry Holtermann and Roy Barton. (Courtesy of John W. Vurckio.)

The old yellow fire engine parked next to the new fire engine flank the firehouse. There are two volunteer fire companies on Staten Island—Richmond Town and Travis. On being a volunteer fireman, Vurckio said: "You either like this or you don't. You have to be willing to get up at two or three in the morning to answer calls." At eighty, he still answers calls uncomplainingly. One of his calls was from the author of this book. Vurckio's usual response? Of course. Despite recent open-heart surgery, he arose from his bed at 7 am to pick up a photograph album from the fire company's secretary, George Wilton Sr., so I could meet him at 11 am to select pictures for the book. (Courtesy of Richmond Engine Company No. 1.)

In an age when people often think there's a lack of community spirit and that nobody does anything for nothing, the volunteer fire company proves them wrong. Pictured here with an old horse-drawn fire vehicle in front of Clove Lake Stables are volunteers getting ready for the annual July Fourth Travis Parade. They include: secretary Arnold Erler (left); Charles Petro (about to mount); Captain Carl Kinn (far right); Robert Merlino (behind Kinn); and William Kili (next to Merlino). The driver is an employee of the stables. (Courtesy of Richmond Engine Company No. 1.)

A 1903 vintage pumper owned by the company recalls a time when firefighting was less "high tech." (Courtesy of Richmond Engine Company No. 1.)

98

"Showtime at St. Andrew's Church, about 1946" is written on the back of this charming photograph of Paralee Neergaard (far left), Jean Anderson (center), and Marguerite Becard. Each dress is a different pastel shade with matching hats. (Collection of Jean Anderson Matula.)

Bettina (Betty) Anderson with the family English setter, Tony, photographed in 1946. The houses in the background are on Center Street. (Collection of Jean Anderson Matula.)

An "after-the-show" party held at the home of Jean Anderson, after a fund-raiser in St. Andrew's Birch Hall. Seated is Jean Anderson. At her right is the late Tom Ryan, at the left is Robert Grant, and standing is Marguerite Becard Meldrum. The photograph was taken c. 1946. (Collection of Jean Anderson Matula.)

100

This photograph of Mr. and Mrs. Oscar Carlson was taken in 1949, in front of 80 Arthur Kill Road, following the christening of their baby daughter Kaaren in St. Andrew's Church. Pictured with the family are the godparents, Jean Anderson and the late Herbert Carlson. (Collection of Jean Anderson Matula.)

An unidentified St. Andrew's Church outing for young people of the parish. The original picture was out of focus, which prevents the reading of the banner held by the gentleman on the right in the white hat. The priest stands in the back row. (Courtesy of St. Andrew's.)

This photograph of Bettina Anderson, Jean's sister, was taken in 1947. (Collection of Jean Anderson Matula.)

Bill Anderson and his wife, Tina, having a wonderful time at a backyard corn roast in 1947. (Collection of Jean Anderson Matula.)

Jim Albus (left), a Latourette golf pro for twenty-five years, and golf-course supervisor Oscar Michaud. In an article in the *Staten Island Advance*, it was written: "Albus had 54 rounds in the 60s in 1994. He finished in the Top 10 in 18 of 35 starts, 11 times in the Top 3. He went five weeks in the Top 5. Twice. Nobody—not Nicklaus or Palmer or Trevino or Floyd—ever made as many birdies in one season." (Courtesy of Oscar Michaud.)

This 1922 photograph shows the Latourette House before its surrounding grounds became a golf course and the house became the clubhouse. The present-day clubhouse porch was added in the 1930s. The Latourettes were an old Staten Island family, though not among the earliest inhabitants. The original Latourette was a French Huguenot who came to America—no one knows what year. In the *Annals of Staten Island* by J.J. Clute, the name was spelled various ways, including La Turrete and Latorette. Located on Richmond Hill Road in the Greenbelt, Latourette is owned by the City of New York and operated by the American Golf Corp. (Source: Leng and Davis.)

The Latourette clubhouse today sits atop 125 acres of developed and 455 acres of wooded parkland. In addition to the elegant, Greek Revival-style house built in 1836, the green was expanded to an 18-hole golf course as part of a 1934 WPA project. The hill was a favorite for skiing and sleighing. (Photograph by T. Navarra.)

Oscar Michaud has been honored for his contributions to Staten Island golfers because of the improvements he initiated while supervisor of Latourette from 1947 to 1967. Michaud was inducted in 1996 into the Staten Island Sports Hall of Fame. "Mich," as he is called, is known to generations of Staten Islanders for his outstanding athletic achievements at Curtis High School and for coaching young people in a variety of sports. At ninety, he is still an avid square dancer. Here Mich checks the turf in a *c.* 1950s photograph. (Courtesy of Oscar Michaud.)

This plaque, on the right side of the Latourette back porch, was donated by the New York Community Trust in 1973. (Photograph by T. Navarra.)

In front of the Latourette porch in the 1950s are, from left to right: Charlie Starte (the citywide director of recreation), Oscar Michaud, and golf pro Paul Spinetta. (Courtesy of Oscar Michaud.)

Ladies out on the green. (Courtesy of Oscar Michaud.)

These winners of the Citywide Golf Pro Championship at Latourette are, from left to right: an unidentified runner-up, Oscar Michaud, and winner Eddie Madjha. The photograph was possibly taken in the 1960s. (Courtesy of Oscar Michaud.)

This golfer appears to need a rescue from the rough. (Courtesy of Oscar Michaud.)

An Easter 1947 photograph of Mrs. William (Tina) Anderson and her daughters, Jean (left) and Betty. The garage, which is no longer standing, was behind their house at 80 Arthur Kill Road, next door to 74 Arthur Kill, now restored as the Parsonage restaurant. The houses in the background are on Center Street. (Collection of Jean Anderson Matula.)

Richmond Fire Company No. 1 staging a rescue. Although the photograph is undated and the people's faces are obscured, the scene rings true both in fact and fiction. (Courtesy of John W. Vurckio.)

Three

Lighthouse Hill

How many romantics have looked at this lighthouse and felt as Rudyard Kipling did: "Airly Beacon, Airly Beacon; Oh the pleasant sight to see Shires and towns from Airly Beacon, While my love climbed up to me!" (Photograph by T. Navarra.)

Today, technological advances have eliminated much of the work of the lighthouse keeper, and in some instances the need for lighthouses altogether. In the early days, when the lighthouse keeper had to operate pumps to create the oil-powered beam, horse-drawn wagons brought the large supplies required to keep the light burning. The keeper lived in a two-family house adjacent to the lighthouse. The home has been sold and substantially renovated as a one-family residence. (Photograph by T. Navarra.)

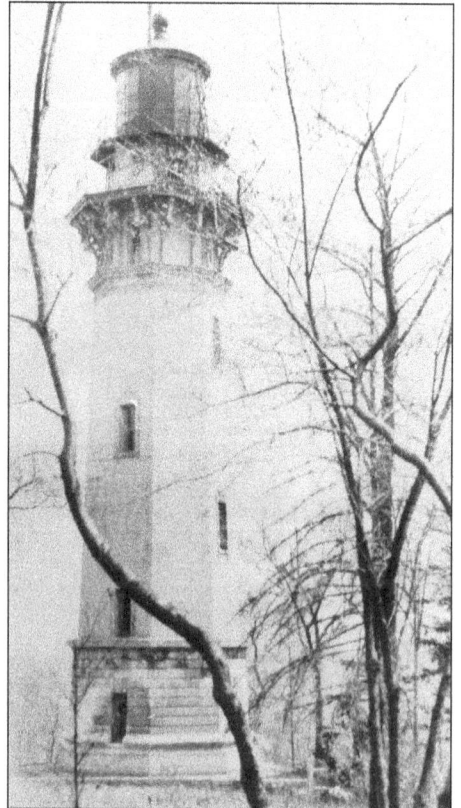

The lighthouse was built in 1912 and set on an octagonal base. The beam has operated continuously since it opened. The beam lined up with West Bank Light, and it is one of the range lights for Ambrose Channel in lower New York Bay. It is visible for 21 miles and continues to maintain an elegant presence on the hill. This view is from a postcard done by P.L. Sperr in 1924. (Collection of the Staten Island Institute of Arts and Sciences, New York.)

Jacques Marchais is the professional name of Jacqueline Klauber, who was born Edna Coblentz in Cincinnati, Ohio, in 1887. An actress in her early life, she performed in many productions under the name Edna Norman. After two failed marriages, she married Harry Klauber and moved to Lighthouse Hill in 1921. Marchais' lifelong love for and fascination with Tibetan art and culture can be traced to her childhood, when she discovered a trunk in the attic and found thirteen Tibetan figurines that her grandfather had brought to this country. She financed the building of the Buddhist museum and religious art collections through her business as a New York art dealer. (Courtesy of the Jacques Marchais Museum of Tibetan Art.)

The Jacques Marchais Museum of Tibetan Art, located on Lighthouse Hill and billed as the only museum dealing exclusively with Tibetan art in the Western world, is the legacy of a unique woman. Composed of two stone buildings designed in 1943 to 1947 to resemble a Buddhist monastery, the museum houses an extensive collection of ritual and religious art objects of the Tibetan and other Eastern cultures. Situated on a beautiful hill overlooking New York Bay, the museum affectionately called "the jewel in the lotus" celebrated its 50th anniversary in 1995. (Courtesy of the Jacques Marchais Museum of Tibetan Art.)

Jacques Marchais sits majestically below the altar in the Tibetan Museum of Art on October 5, 1947, the day of a grand dedication ceremony to mark the opening of the museum to the public. *Life* magazine covered the opening in its December 8, 1947 issue. Jacques Marchais realized her dream, but died on February 15, 1948, followed shortly by her husband, Harry. A neighbor and friend, Helen A. Watkins, took charge. The museum and its collections were maintained through the efforts of supporters. New York State Senator John J. Marchi helped obtain a grant for the museum. Barbara Lipton, a curator with extensive museum experience, accepted the position of full-time director. (Courtesy of the Jacques Marchais Museum of Tibetan Art.)

The *Hayagriva*, an eighteenth-century Mongolian figurine, portrays a deity important both for meditation and protection against disease. Barbara Lipton has written a book, *Treasures of Tibetan Art*, to be published by Oxford University Press. The book deals with highlights of the museum collection. This photograph is by Geoffrey Clements. (Courtesy of the Jacques Marchais Museum of Tibetan Art.)

This drawing of the front entrance of the Jacques Marchais Museum of Tibetan Art, at 338 Lighthouse Avenue, was done by Norman Morrison. Museum hours are 1 to 5 pm, Wednesday through Sunday, April to November. (Courtesy of the Jacques Marchais Museum of Tibetan Art.)

Buddhist monks from Howell, NJ, photographed by Barbara Lipton, visit the Tibetan Museum in the Lighthouse Hill section of Staten Island. (Courtesy of the Jacques Marchais Museum of Tibetan Art.)

The beautiful gardens and terraces were designed by Jacques Marchais. She worked with stonemason Joseph Premiano and used an old car to haul stones up the hill for the building and the garden. (Photograph by Margaret Lundrigan Ferrer.)

In 1991, His Holiness, the 14th Dalai Lama, the spiritual head of Lamaism (the Mahayana Buddhism of Tibet and Mongolia), visited the museum and said: "I think the Tibetan culture essentially provides us with a more peaceful nature. Therefore, when Tibetans are passing through a difficult period, the Tibetan mental state is, generally speaking, quite peaceful. So I consider that something really important . . . and worthwhile to preserve." He added that at the museum, he felt as if he were in Tibet. Barbara Lipton accompanies him. (Courtesy of the Jacques Marchais Museum of Tibetan Art.)

The Dalai Lama's speech on the museum's opening day complimented the efforts of Jacques Marchais: "There is real danger of the disappearance of the unique Tibetan culture. So at such a time, this kind of work is very, very useful . . . I feel that I see part of a Tibetan antique collection, ancient Tibetan things. I find that the idea for setting up this kind of museum as early as the early 1900s was quite remarkable." Hon. John J. Marchi and His Holiness bow to each other in a traditional Buddhist greeting. Barbara Lipton is in the center. (Courtesy of the Jacques Marchais Museum of Tibetan Art.)

Another view of the Jacques Marchais Museum of Tibetan Art, at that time known as the Jacques Marchais Center of Tibetan Art. On the museum's golden anniversary, the staff created a program that offered a brief history: "The collections of the museum consist primarily of sculptures and paintings from Tibet, Mongolia and Northern China, dating from the 15th to the early 20th century, and include excellent examples of 18th-century Chinese cloisonne from the workshops of Emperor Qienlong. The majority of items were obtained by Jacques Marchais from the mid-'30s to the mid-'40s. Since 1985, several hundred objects, *thangkas* and photographs have been added to the collections through gifts and occasional purchases." (Courtesy of the Jacques Marchais Museum of Tibetan Art.)

Carl Michael Eger, Norwegian-born architect, came to the United States in 1869 and in 1876 founded the Hecla Architectural Iron Works. In 1888, the firm designed and built the 100-foot, double-spiral iron staircases for the Statue of Liberty. The Egers were childless, and when Carl died on May 19, 1916, at the age of seventy-two, he left an estate of more than $1 million, with $60,000 designated for the care of elderly Norwegians. (Courtesy of the Eger Home.)

Eger's house on 112–14 Pulaski Street, Brooklyn, was converted to the first Eger Norwegian Lutheran Home for the Aged, Inc. Although Carl Eger had left two other homes for this purpose, they proved unsuitable as communal dwellings. As an alternative, his sister, Catherine Eger, made Carl's lavishly furnished residence available for elderly in need of care. News of the *Eger Gamle Hjem* spread quickly in the Norwegian community, and soon the enormous number of elderly in need exceeded the space available. (Courtesy of the Eger Home.)

117

The Eger Home moved to Staten Island in 1926 in response to the growing need for a larger facility. The "White House," located on Lighthouse Hill in the Egbertville section of Staten Island, was built in 1830 as a finishing school for girls. Before it was purchased by Eger, it had also functioned as the Aldrich Farm Community, as well as a convalescent home for boys aged twelve to twenty who were recuperating from surgery. The home continued its farming activities, which contributed to the maintenance of the community. This is a photograph of the "White House," *c.* 1935, with flags flying. (Courtesy of the Eger Home.)

Catherine Eger, one of the first members of the board of trustees and one of the eight incorporators of the Eger Home, assisted Pastor Charles S. Everson. She saw to it that the Carl Michael Eger Home became functional. (Courtesy of the Eger Home.)

Harper's Weekly, dated July 31, 1888, printed an illustration of the spiral iron staircases designed by Eger's Hecla Architectural Iron Works for the Statue of Liberty. (Courtesy of the Eger Home.)

Pastor Charles S. Everson, of Our Savior's Lutheran Church, had been Carl Michael Eger's long-time pastor. He was elected chairman of the board of directors of the Eger Norwegian Home for the Aged. Tireless in his efforts to bring the home into being, he served from 1916 to 1918. (Courtesy of the Eger Home.)

The Eger "family," *c.* 1935, in front of the "White House." (Courtesy of the Eger Home.)

In the booklet, *Eger: A History of Caring,* Reverend Paul A. Qualben, MD, writes: "On July 5, 1916, the application for incorporation of the Eger Home was approved. The final filing of the incorporation in Albany and in King's County (Brooklyn) was completed on October 31, 1916—the formal beginning of Eger's institutional life." Shown here is the certificate of incorporation signed by William R. Stewart, president of the State of New York State Board of Charities. (Courtesy of the Eger Home.)

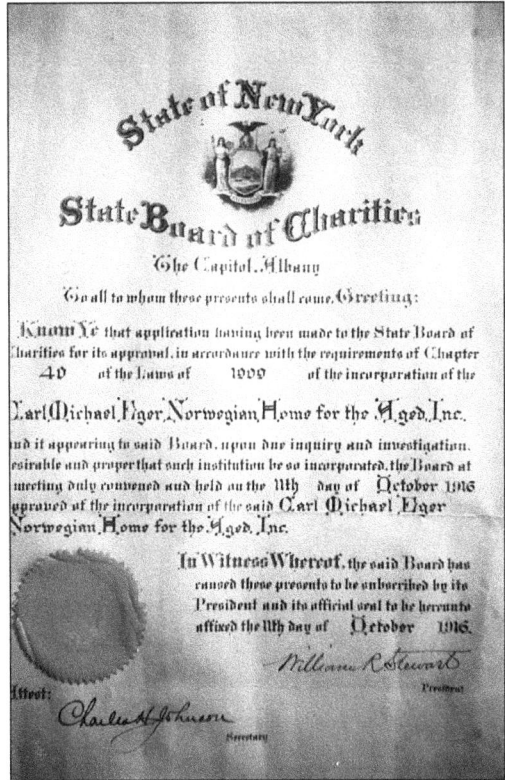

One of the rooms of the "White House," occupied by elderly residents in 1926. A large portrait of Carl Michael Eger is set on a chair near the fireplace. (Courtesy of the Eger Home.)

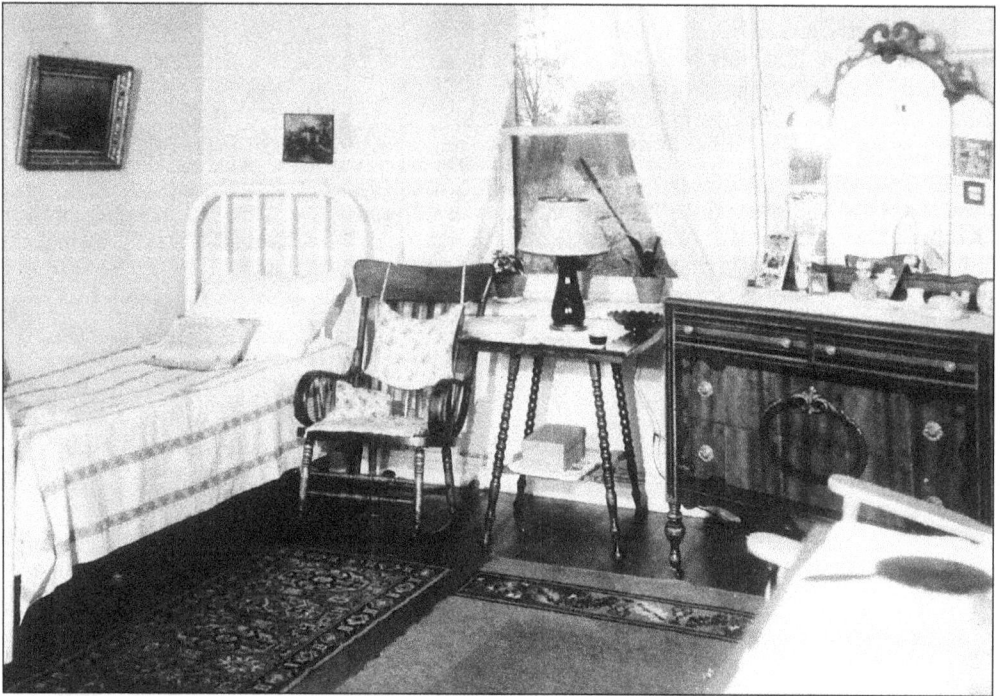
One of the bedrooms at the Eger Home. (Courtesy of the Eger Home.)

This interior shot points out the elegance and comfort of the Eger Home. (Courtesy of the Eger Home.)

The Eger Home's serene dining room betrays nothing of the incredible effort it took for the Eger staff to care for the long-lived Norwegians. Without government assistance such as our modern Medicare and Medicaid, the Eger Home persisted with the generous contributions of Catherine Eger, community churches and organizations, members of the board, and volunteer help. After various expansions, the Eger Home now has 378 beds and is respected for its holistic care and compassion. (Courtesy of the Eger Home.)

American architect Frank Lloyd Wright designed "Crimson Beech," the only private residence designed by Wright in New York City. When William Cass, vice-president of a New York personnel agency, and his wife Catherine decided to commission a Frank Lloyd Wright house, they embarked on a sometimes arduous, always fun, and ultimately rewarding labor of love. (Courtesy of Catherine Cass.)

Throughout the years, "Crimson Beech" has been a source of interest for Frank Lloyd Wright enthusiasts and architects alike. This rendering was done by D. Korves of the southeast elevation—200 feet above sea level on Lighthouse Hill. Horizontal battens, horizontally accentuated brick work, and typical "Prairie" eaves create the mood of a building hugging the ground. Wright's organic architecture combines nature and structure. In 1959, the Cass family moved in. Since then, they have been excellent stewards of this architectural treasure and have both preserved the home and made it available for the purpose of architectural and academic study. (Courtesy of Catherine Cass.)

The living room furnishings are mainly Wright's design. A man of wit, wisdom, and colossal nerve, Wright believed that the architect should not only design the building but its accessories as well. As he put it: "I prefer honest arrogance to hypocritical humility." Even the Schumacher draperies are the "Wright" choice." (Courtesy of Catherine Cass.)

In one of the bedrooms of "Crimson Beech," situated off the long gallery with its cabinets and windows, batten strips of Philippine mahogany paneling carry through the clean lines of Frank Lloyd Wright's design. Macy's and General Electric worked together to achieve the architect's vision of the home. Mrs. Cass said she refused an offer made for her home because the prospective buyer wanted to remove the interior mahogany and outside put up a black gate to the property. (Photograph by Jim Romano, courtesy of Catherine Cass.)

Mrs. Cass purchased four paintings—one for each season—of her home. This winter scene accentuates the sleek lines and sumptuous setting of the house. (Courtesy of Catherine Cass.)

"Crimson Beech," named for the beautiful tree which graced the property, has remained remarkably unchanged. The Cass family has meticulously maintained its integrity, and the house received an award from the Frank Lloyd Wright Conservancy. It is also registered as a New York City landmark. The tree was actually a copper beech, but Mr. Cass informally "renamed" it because of its fiery red leaves. (Photograph by Andrew's Photograph Shop, December 6, 1961, courtesy of Catherine Cass.)

The ancient copper beech tree fell during a hurricane in 1967. Another has been planted in its place. (Courtesy of Catherine Cass.)

William and Catherine Cass stand at the pool, built during the 1960s following a series of brush fires as a way to protect the house from future fires in the wooded area. This September 14, 1976 photograph was taken by Jim Romano. (Courtesy of Catherine Cass.)

Bibliography

Clute, John J. *Annals of Staten Island from Its Discovery to the Present Time.* New York: Press of Charles Vogt, 1877.

Davis, William T. *Days Afield on Staten Island.* The Staten Island Institute of Arts and Sciences commemorative edition, 1994.

Davis, William T.; Charles W. Leng, and Royden W. Vosburgh. *The Church of St. Andrew, Staten Island, Its History, Vital Records and Gravestone Inscriptions.* Staten Island: Staten Island Historical Society, 1925.

Heil, Dorothy Marks. "The Holtermann Family." unpublished, November 1974.

Qualben, Paul A., MD. *Eger: A History of Caring.* Staten Island: The Eger Group, 1991.

Sachs, Charles L. *Made on Staten Island: Agriculture, Industry and Suburban Living in the City.* Staten Island: Staten Island Historical Society, 1988.

Steinmeyer, Henry G. *Staten Island 1524–1898.* Staten Island: Staten Island Historical Society, 1950.

www.ingramcontent.com/pod-product-compliance
Lightning Source LLC
Chambersburg PA
CBHW080906100426
42812CB00007B/2177